Contemplative Prayers

for use with Anglican Prayer Beads

by Tami Allen

CONTENTS

PREFACE

When I first heard of Anglican Prayer Beads, my Protestant, Evangelical upbringing screamed in opposition to another boring, empty, formulaic ritual to be performed. "Shun vain repetitions." I didn't want to be a "white-washed Pharisee."

In His merciful kindness and grace, God took me beyond my personal bias and led me on a contemplative spiritual journey. I learned that these prayer beads are neither mindless nor mystical, but simply a tool that helps me quiet my spirit and enter into His presence. The anchoring touch of the beads helps keep my mind from wandering during prayer time.

Certain worship songs, repeated again and again, intense prayer times with my Bible study group or even a quiet walk in the woods — each of these have taken me to a place of quietness and resting at His feet. In much the same way, praying with my prayer beads allows me to focus my thoughts and "be still and know that He is God."

My prayer is that you, too, will find this method of prayer to be an effective way to slow down the hurried rhythm of your life. May you find that inner sanctuary, a place of peaceful refreshment and spiritual transformation at the feet of our Savior.

Yet give attention to your servant's prayer and his plea for mercy, O Lord my God. Hear the cry and the prayer that your servant is praying in your presence this day.
1 Kings 8:28 (NIV)

The History of Prayer Beads

Throughout history, repetitious prayers and the use of counters (beads, pebbles, knots in string, etc.) have been widespread in religious traditions. In early times a person would put pebbles in their pocket in the morning and throughout the day they would drop a pebble each time they prayed. It became customary to tie knots in strings. Later, beads were made of fruit pits, dried berries, pieces of bone or bits of dried clay. Wealthier folks would use gems and jewels or gold nuggets.

The Christian rosary has been traced to the Crusaders who perhaps adopted the use of beads from the Arabs, who may have seen them in India. Today's Anglican prayer beads are a relatively new form of prayer that has been adopted from the prayer rope of the Orthodox church and the rosary of the Catholic church. They were developed in the mid 1980's by Rev. Lynn Bauman with the help of her contemplative prayer group.

Symbolism of the Beads

The Invitatory bead is meant to invite you into His presence. The four Cruciform beads form a cross and divide the Week beads. The Week beads are made up of twenty-eight beads divided into four groups of seven. The Weeks symbolize the seven days of creation, the temporal week, the seasons of the church year and the seven sacraments. In the Judeo-Christian tradition the number seven represents spiritual perfection and completion. The total number of beads is thirty-three, the number of years in Jesus' earthly life.

Why use Prayer Beads?

They offer a focal point, a way of keeping the mind from wandering while praying. They bring a physical or kinesthetic aspect to prayer; something to hold on to.

Suggestions for Using This Prayer Book

The prayers included in this book have been adapted from scriptures and songs. Some are repetitive, some are successive, others give you space to insert your name, the name of someone for whom you want to pray, or an issue you want to bring before the Lord. You can use these prepared prayers or compose your own. They are intended to be suggestions to aid you, not mindless rituals with magical results. Simply reciting the words will not bring about spiritual growth. It is the intentions of your heart, not absentminded mutterings, that God notices. Some people have found that even just holding the beads (without progressing bead-by-bead) assists them in focusing during their prayer time.

Praying with the Beads

To begin, decide which prayers you want to assign to the Cross and each of the beads. Hold the Cross and say the prayer you have assigned to it, then move to the Invitatory Bead. Then enter the circle of the prayer with the first Cruciform bead. Moving to the right, go through the first set of seven beads to the next Cruciform bead, continue around the circle, saying the prayers for each bead. Repeat the circle as many times as you like. After the final Cruciform bead, you will exit by moving to the Invitatory Bead and then the cross.

Pray around the circle of beads in an unhurried pace. Pause and reflect as the Holy Spirit prompts you. Allow your mind to rest and your heart to become quiet and still.

A period of silence should follow the prayer, for a time of reflection and listening. Listening is an important part of all prayer.

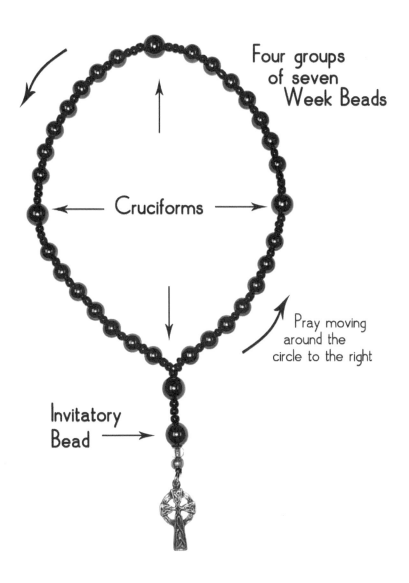

Four groups
of seven
Week Beads

Cruciforms

Pray moving
around the
circle to the right

Invitatory
Bead

Psalm 145

Cross: Great are You, Lord, and greatly to be praised; Your greatness is unsearchable.

Invitatory Bead: I will meditate on the glorious splendor of Your majesty and on Your wondrous works.

Cruciform Beads: All Your works shall praise You, O Lord, and Your saints shall bless You.

Week Beads:
1. You are gracious and full of compassion, slow to anger and great in mercy
2. You are good to all, and Your tender mercies are over all Your works
3. Your kingdom is an everlasting kingdom and Your dominion endures throughout all generations
4. You uphold all who fall and raise up all who are bowed down
5. You open Your hand and satisfy the desire of every living thing
6. You are righteous in all Your ways, gracious in all Your works
7. You are near to all who call upon You in truth

Exit Invitatory Bead: My mouth will speak Your praise, and all flesh shall bless Your holy name forever and ever.

Exit Cross: Great are You, Lord, and greatly to be praised; Your greatness is unsearchable.

Philippians 4

Cross: I will be anxious for nothing, but in everything, by prayer and supplication with thanksgiving, I will let my requests be made known to You, O God.

Invitatory Bead: The peace of God, which surpasses all understanding, will guard my heart and mind through Christ Jesus.

Cruciform Beads: I will meditate on these things

Week Beads:
1. Whatever things are true and noble
2. Whatever things are just
3. Whatever things are pure
4. Whatever things are lovely
5. Whatever things are of good report
6. If there is any virtue
7. If there is anything praiseworthy

Exit Invitatory Bead: The things which I have learned and received from You, these will I do.

Exit Cross: The God of peace will be with me.

Psalm 139

Cross: Search me, O God, and know my heart. Try me and know my anxieties; and see if there is any wicked way in me.

Invitatory Bead: Lead me in the way everlasting.

Cruciform Beads: How precious are Your thoughts toward me, O God!

Week Beads:
1. You have looked deep into my heart, Lord, and You know all about me.
2. You know when I am resting or when I am working
3. You understand my thoughts from far away
4. You see me whether I am working or resting
5. You know all my ways very well
6. Before I even speak a word, You know what I will say
7. With Your powerful arm You protect me from every side

Exit Invitatory Bead: Your infinite knowledge is too wonderful for me. It is too much for me to understand.

Exit Cross: I praise You because I am fearfully and wonderfully made.

Ephesians 1

Cross: In Christ I have redemption through His blood and the forgiveness of my sins.

Invitatory Bead: Praise be to the God and Father of our Lord Jesus Christ, who has blessed me in the heavenly realms with every spiritual blessing in Christ.

Cruciform Beads: These are the things I ask of the God of our Lord Jesus Christ, the glorious Father.

Week Beads:
1. Give me the Spirit of wisdom and revelation
2. I desire to know You better
3. Enlighten the eyes of my heart
4. Teach me the hope to which You have called me
5. Let me see the riches of Your glorious inheritance in Your people
6. Reveal to me Your incomparably great power for those who believe
7. Show me the resurrection power that is far above all rule and authority, power, dominion and names

Exit Invitatory Bead: I am Your workmanship, created in Christ Jesus for good works.

Exit Cross: Peace, love with faith and grace are mine through Christ Jesus.

Ephesians 3

Cross: I bow in prayer before the Father.

Invitatory Bead: It is from Him that every family in heaven and on earth has its name.

Cruciform Beads: God is able to do immeasurably more than all we ask or imagine, according to His power that is at work in us.

Week Beads: (*Fill in the blank with "me or I" or the name of another person*)
1. I ask You to strengthen _____ by Your Spirit — not a brute strength, but a glorious inner strength
2. I pray that Christ may live in _____ heart by faith
3. I pray that _____ will be filled with love
4. I pray that _____ will be able to understand how wide and long and high and deep Your love is
5. That _____ may really come to know practically the love of Christ which surpasses all knowledge
6. That _____ may be filled through all _____ being with the fullness of God
7. That _____ may become a body wholly filled and flooded with God Himself

Exit Invitatory Bead: May the Holy Spirit Himself dwell in _____ innermost being.

Exit Cross: To Him be glory in the church and in Christ Jesus throughout all generations forever and ever! Amen!

Psalm 37

Cross: My steps are ordered by You, Lord.

Invitatory Bead: Those who wait on the Lord shall inherit the earth.

Cruciform Beads: My salvation is from the Lord.

Week Beads:
1. I will not fret because of evil doers
2. Nor be envious of the workers of iniquity
3. I trust in You, Lord
4. I dwell in the land
5. And feed on Your faithfulness
6. I delight myself in You, Lord
7. And You will give me the desires of my heart

Alternate Week Beads:
1. I commit my way to the Lord
2. And trust also in You
3. I rest in You, Lord
4. And wait patiently for You
5. I cease from anger
6. And forsake wrath
7. I will not fret - it only causes harm

Exit Invitatory Bead: My future is peace.

Exit Cross: You, O Lord, help me and deliver me.

Be Still

Cross: God is my refuge and strength, a very present help in trouble.

Invitatory Bead: I will meditate within my heart on my bed, and be still.

Cruciform Beads: You have loved me with an everlasting love.

Week Beads: I will be still and know that You are God.

Exit Invitatory Bead: I will dwell in a peaceful habitation, in a secure dwelling, and in quiet resting places.

Exit Cross: The Lord of hosts is with me; the God of Jacob is my refuge.

Scripture References:

Psalm 46:7	Psalm 4:4	Psalm 46:10
Isaiah 32:18	Psalm 46:11	Jeremiah 31:3

God is Able

Cross: I will draw near to God and He will draw near to me.

Invitatory Bead: I will not fear, for You have redeemed me; I am Yours.

Cruciform Beads: Speak, Lord, for your servant is listening.

Week Beads: (*Add a name or issue in the blank—it can be the same for each bead, different for each bead or different for each week.*)
You are able and you can be trusted with _____

Exit Invitatory Bead: I will not fear, for You have redeemed me and I am Yours.

Exit Cross: I have drawn near to You, O God, and You have drawn near to me.

Scripture References:
James 4:8   Isaiah 43:1   1 Samuel 3:10

Prayer of Renewal

Cross: You are my place of quiet retreat; I wait for Your Word to renew me.

Invitatory Bead: This hope I have as an anchor of my soul, a hope both sure and steadfast and one which enters within the veil.

Cruciform Beads: Return me to Yourself, O Lord, and I shall be restored. Renew my days as of old.

Week Beads:
1. Create in me a clean heart, O God
2. Renew a steadfast spirit within me
3. Do not cast me away from Your presence
4. Do not take Your Holy Spirit from me
5. Restore to me the joy of Your salvation
6. Uphold me by Your generous Spirit
7. Then I will teach transgressors Your ways, and sinners shall be converted to You

Exit Invitatory Bead: I will not be conformed to this world, but transformed by the renewing of my mind, that I may prove what is that good and acceptable and perfect will of God.

Exit Cross: When I wait upon the Lord, I shall renew my strength.

Scripture References:

Psalm 119:114	Hebrews 6:19	Lamentations 5:21
Psalm 51:10-13	Romans 12:2	Isaiah 40:31

God's Guidance

Cross: I will call on Your name and You will answer me; You will say, "You are My child," and I will say, "The Lord is my God."

Invitatory Bead: You are near to all who call upon You, to all who call upon You in truth.

Cruciform Beads: Send me Your light and Your faithful care, let them lead me.

Week Beads:
1. Wisdom will enter my heart
2. Knowledge will be pleasant to my soul
3. Discretion will preserve me
4. Understanding will keep me
5. To deliver me from the way of evil
6. So I may walk in the way of goodness
7. And keep to the paths of righteousness

Exit Invitatory: Wisdom rests in the heart of him who has understanding.

Exit Cross: I will submit to God and be at peace with Him; in this way prosperity will come to me. I will accept instruction from His mouth and lay up His words in my heart.

Scripture References:
Zechariah 13:9   Psalm 145:18   Psalm 43:3
Proverbs 2:10-12, 20 Proverbs 14:33   Job 22:21-22

His Presence

Cross: I will enter His gates with thanksgiving in my heart and into His courts with praise.

Invitatory Bead: When I was really hurting, I prayed to the Lord; He answered my prayer, and took my worries away.

Cruciform Beads: I have made You, the Most High, my refuge and my dwelling place.

Week Beads:
1. You are my refuge and my fortress, my God, in You will I trust
2. In Your presence is fullness of joy
3. The upright dwell in Your presence
4. Strength and gladness are in Your presence
5. You hide me in the secret place of Your presence
6. I will be silent at Your presence, oh Lord God
7. You present me faultless before the presence of Your glory with exceeding joy

Exit Invitatory Bead: Blessed are those who dwell in Your house.

Exit Cross: Lord, You have said, "My Presence will go with you, and I will give you rest."

Scripture References:

Psalm 100:4	Psalm 118:5	Psalm 91:9
Psalm 91:2	Psalm 16:8	Psalm 140:13
2 Chronicles 16:27	Psalm 31:20	Zephaniah 1:7
Jude 24	Psalm 84:4	Exodus 33:14

Prayer of Refreshing

Cross: I am blessed when I hunger and thirst for righteousness for I will be filled.

Invitatory Bead: I repent and ask You to blot out all my sins so that times of refreshing may come from Your presence, oh Lord.

Cruciform Beads: I will cast my burden upon the Lord, and He will sustain me.

Week Beads: In returning and rest I am saved, quietness and confidence are my strength.

Exit Invitatory Bead: Your kindness will not depart from me, nor will Your covenant of peace be removed.

Exit Cross: You are the Lord who has mercy on me.

Scripture References:

Matthew 5:6	Acts 3:19	Psalm 55:22
Isaiah 30:15	Isaiah 54:10	

Prayer for Rest

Cross: Be merciful to me, O God, be merciful to me! For my soul trusts in You; and in the shadow of Your wings I will make my refuge.

Invitatory Bead: I come with You by myself to a quiet place to get some rest.

Cruciform Beads: I rest in the Lord and wait patiently for Him.

Week Beads:
1. I come to You as I labor and I'm heavy laden
2. You give me rest
3. I take your yoke upon me
4. I learn from You
5. You are gentle and lowly in heart
6. I find rest for my soul
7. Your yoke is easy and Your burden is light

Exit Invitatory Bead: As a believer, I enter Your rest, a rest that remains for Your people.

Exit Cross: Your people will live in peaceful dwelling places, in secure homes, in undisturbed places of rest.

Scripture References:

Psalm 57:1	Mark 6:31	Psalm 37:7
Matthew 11:28-30	Hebrews 4:3, 9	Isaiah 32:18

God My Protector

Cross: God is my refuge and strength, a very present help in trouble, therefore I will not fear.

Invitatory Bead: I will come boldly to the throne of grace to receive mercy and find grace to help in time of need.

Cruciform Beads: I trust in the Lord; He is my deliverer and protector.

Week Beads:
1. I lift up my eyes to the mountains— where my help comes from
2. My help comes from the Lord who made heaven and earth
3. You will not allow my foot to be moved
4. You will not slumber
5. You are my keeper
6. You protect me from all evil
7. You preserve my soul

Exit Invitatory Bead: The Lord shall protect my going out and my coming in from this time forth and even forevermore.

Exit Cross: God is my refuge and strength, a very present help in trouble, therefore I will not fear.

Scripture References:
Psalm 46:1-2   Hebrews 4:16   Psalm 115:11
Psalm 121

Wait for the Lord

Cross: The Lord is in His holy temple, let all the earth keep silence before Him.

Invitatory Bead: Those who wait upon the Lord shall renew their strength.

Cruciform Beads: I will hear what God the LORD will speak, for He will speak peace to His people.

Week Beads:
1. Cause me to hear Your lovingkindness in the morning
2. For in You do I trust
3. Cause me to know the way in which I should walk
4. For I lift up my soul to You
5. Deliver me, O Lord, from my enemies; in You I take shelter
6. Revive me, O Lord, for Your name's sake
7. For Your righteousness' sake bring my soul out of trouble

Exit Invitatory Bead: The Lord is good to those who wait for Him, to the soul who seeks Him.

Exit Cross: It is good that one should hope and wait quietly for the salvation of the Lord.

Scripture References:
Habakkuk 2:20   Isaiah 40:31   Lamentations 3:25-26
Psalm 143:8-11   Psalm 85:8

Prayer of Hope

Cross: Let Your mercy be upon me, O Lord, just as I have hope in You.

Invitatory Bead: Why are you cast down, O my soul? And why are you disquieted within me? Hope in God, for I shall yet praise Him for the help of His countenance.

Cruciform Beads: I will be of good courage, and He will strengthen my heart because I hope in the Lord.

Week Beads:
1. I will bless the Lord who has given me counsel
2. My heart also instructs me in the night seasons
3. I have set the Lord always before me
4. Because He is at my right hand, I shall not be moved
5. Therefore my heart is glad
6. My glory rejoices
7. My flesh will also rest in hope

Exit Invitatory Bead: I gird up the loins of my mind, I am sober, and I rest my hope fully in Your grace.

Exit Cross: God of hope, fill me with all joy and peace in believing that I may abound in hope by the power of the Holy Spirit.

Scripture References:

Psalm 33:22	Psalm 42:5	Psalm 31:24
Psalm 16:7-9	1 Peter 1:13	Romans 15:13

God, My Helper

Cross: Those who trust, lean on, and confidently hope in the Lord are as Mount Zion, which cannot be moved, but abides and stands fast forever.

Invitatory Bead: As the mountains are round about Jerusalem, so You, Lord, are round about me from this time forth and forever.

Cruciform Beads: Behold, God is my helper.

Week Beads:
1. In the day when I cried out, You answered me
2. Though I walk in the midst of trouble, You will revive me
3. You will stretch forth Your hand against the wrath of my enemies
4. Your right hand will save me
5. You will accomplish what concerns me
6. Your lovingkindness, O Lord, is everlasting
7. You will not forsake the works of Your hands

Exit Invitatory Bead: I will say to the Lord, "You are my refuge and my fortress; My God, in You will I trust.

Exit Cross: The Lord is on my side; I will not fear.

Scripture References:

Psalm 125:1-2	Psalm 54:4	Psalm 138:3, 7-8
Psalm 91:2	Psalm 118:6	

You Know Me

Cross: Give ear to my words, O Lord, and consider my sighing.

Invitatory Bead: Listen to my cry for help, my King and my God, for to You do I pray.

Cruciform Beads: You have redeemed me; You have summoned me by name; I am Yours.

Week Beads:
1. O Lord, You have examined my heart and know everything about me
2. You know my rising and my resting
3. You know my thoughts even when I'm far away
4. You are intimately acquainted with all my ways
5. You know what I am going to say even before I say it, Lord
6. With Your powerful arm You protect me on every side
7. You place Your hand of blessing on my head

Exit Invitatory Bead: God is my refuge and strength, a very present help in trouble. Therefore I will not fear.

Exit Cross: I will be still and know that You are God.

Scripture References:

Psalm 5:1-2	Psalm 139:1-5	Isaiah 43:1
Psalm 46:1-2	Psalm 46:10	

Wisdom from Heaven

Cross: To God belong wisdom and power; counsel and understanding are Yours.

Invitatory Bead: You desire truth in the inward parts, and in the hidden part You will make me to know wisdom.

Cruciform Beads: As I please You, You give wisdom, knowledge and happiness.

Week Beads: The wisdom that comes from heaven is:
1. Pure
2. Peace-loving
3. Considerate
4. Submissive
5. Full of mercy
6. And good fruit
7. Impartial and sincere

Exit Invitatory: Oh, the depth of the riches of Your wisdom and knowledge, O God! How unsearchable are Your judgments, and Your paths are beyond tracing out!

Exit Cross: To the only God, my Savior be glory, majesty, power and authority, through Jesus Christ my Lord, before all ages, now and forevermore! Amen.

Scripture References:

Job 12:13	Psalm 51:6	Ecclesiastes 2:26
James 3	Romans 11:33	Jude 1:25

Prayer of Jabez

Cross: I will not be anxious about anything, but in everything, by prayer and petition, with thanksgiving, I present my requests to You.

Invitatory Bead: You, oh Lord my God, will turn every curse into a blessing for me because You love me.

Cruciform Beads: I shall receive a blessing from You, oh Lord, and righteousness from the God of my salvation.

Week Beads:
1. Oh that You would bless me indeed
2. Enlarge my territory
3. May Your hand be with me
4. I ask that You keep me from all evil
5. May I not cause pain
6. Oh Lord, this is the cry of my heart
7. Lord, grant what I have requested

Exit Invitatory Bead: I have put my entire trust in You, Jesus. Therefore I can live as I was meant to live--and everyone in my house included!

Exit Cross: You will command the blessing upon me in all that I put my hand to, and You will bless me in the land which You give me.

Scripture References:

Philippians 4:6	Deuteronomy 23:5	Psalm 24:5
1 Chronicles 4:10	Acts 16:31	Deuteronomy 28:8

The Fruit of the Spirit

Cross: Father I pray that You would pour out Your Spirit upon me.

Invitatory Bead: I have not received the spirit of the world but the Spirit who is from God, that I may understand what God has freely given me.

Cruciform Beads: If I live by the Spirit, let me also walk by the Spirit.

Week Beads: Lord, let me develop more of the fruit of Your Spirit:
1. love and joy
2. peace and patience
3. kindness
4. goodness
5. faithfulness
6. gentleness
7. self-control

Exit Invitatory Bead: The Spirit of the Lord will rest on me.

Exit Cross: As I live to please the Spirit, from the Spirit I will reap eternal life.

Scripture References:
Joel 2:28   1 Corinthians 2:12   Galatians 5:22, 25
Isaiah 11:2   Galatians 6:8

The Names of the Lord

Cross: I will praise the name of the Lord: for Your name alone is excellent; Your glory is above the earth and heaven.

Invitatory Bead: From the rising of the sun to the place where it sets, the name of the Lord is to be praised.

Cruciform Beads: Some trust in chariots and some in horses, but I trust in the name of the Lord my God.

Week Beads: Lord, You are:
1. El Shaddai — The All-Sufficient One
2. El Olam — Everlasting God
3. Jehovah-Rophe — The Lord that Heals
4. Jehovah Jireh — The Lord will Provide
5. Jehovah-Shalom — The Lord is Peace
6. Jehovah Shammah — The Lord Is There
7. Jehovah Tsidkenu — God our Righteousness

Exit Invitatory: I will praise You, O Lord my God, with all my heart, and I will glorify Your name forevermore.

Exit Cross: At the name of Jesus every knee shall bow, in heaven and on earth and under the earth, and every tongue acknowledge that Jesus Christ is Lord, to the glory of God the Father.

Scripture References:

Psalm 148:13	Psalm 113:3	Psalm 20:7
Genesis 17:1	Exodus 17:15	Exodus 15:26
Philippians 4:19	Judges 6:24	Ezekiel 48:35
Psalm 86:9	Philippians 2:10	Genesis 21:33
Jeremiah 23:5		

Prayer in the Seasons

Cross: All of my life, in every season, You are still God.

Invitatory Bead: I have a reason to sing. I have a reason to worship.

Cruciform Bead 1: This is my prayer in the desert, "My God is the God who provides."

Week 1 Beads:
1. I will bring praise
2. I will bring praise
3. No weapon formed against me shall remain
4. I will rejoice
5. I will declare
6. God is my victory
7. He is here

Cruciform Bead 2: This is my prayer in the fire, "Refine me, Lord through the flames."

Week 2 Beads:
1. I will bring praise
2. I will bring praise
3. No weapon formed against me shall remain
4. I will rejoice
5. I will declare
6. God is my victory
7. He is here

Cruciform Bead 3: This is my prayer in the battle, "I'm a conqueror and co-heir with Christ.

Week 3 Beads:
1. I will bring praise
2. I will bring praise
3. No weapon formed against me shall remain
4. I will rejoice
5. I will declare
6. God is my victory
7. He is here

Cruciform Bead 4: This is my prayer in the harvest, "The seeds I've received I will sow."

Week 4 Beads:
1. I will bring praise
2. I will bring praise
3. No weapon formed against me shall remain
4. I will rejoice
5. I will declare
6. God is my victory
7. He is here

Exit Invitatory Bead: I have a reason to sing. I have a reason to worship.

Exit Cross: All of my life, in every season, You are still God.

Based on: *Desert Song*, by Brooke Fraser, ©2008 Hillsong Music Australia

Prayer for Fasting

Cross: "Now, therefore," says the Lord, "Turn to Me with all Your heart, with fasting, with weeping, and with mourning. So rend your heart and not your garments, return to the Lord your God."

Invitatory Bead: Lord, let this fast be appointed by You, set apart for You, to worship You, honor You, and glorify You, to accomplish Your sovereign will.

Cruciform Beads: This is the fast that You, O Lord have chosen:

Week Beads:
1. To loosen the bonds of wickedness and undo the heavy burdens
2. To let the oppressed go free and break every yoke
3. To share my bread with the hungry and my home with the poor who are outcast
4. To cover the naked and not hide myself from my own flesh
5. Then my light will break forth like the morning and my healing will spring forth speedily
6. My righteousness will go before me and the glory of the Lord will be my rear guard
7. Then I will call and You will answer; I will cry and You will say, "Here I am"

Alternate Weeks:
1. To take away the pointing finger and speaking wickedness
2. To extend my soul to the hungry and satisfy the afflicted soul
3. To build the old waste places and raise up the foundations of many generations
4. To keep my feet from turning away on the Sabbath, from doing my pleasure on Your holy day.
5. To honor You by not doing my own ways, nor finding my own pleasures, nor speaking my own words
6. You, O Lord, will continually guide me, satisfy my soul in drought, and strengthen my bones
7. I will be like a watered garden, like a spring of water whose waters do not fail.

Exit Invitatory Bead: I will delight myself in You, O Lord, and You will cause me to ride on the high hills of the earth and feed me with the heritage of Jacob.

Exit Cross: The mouth of the Lord has spoken.

Scripture References:
Joel 2:12   Isaiah 58:6-14

The Lord is My Safe Place

Cross: You are my Lord. All the good things I have come from You.

Invitatory Bead: I will give honor and thanks to the Lord Who has told me what to do.

Cruciform Beads: My future is in Your hands.

Week Beads:
1. I have placed the Lord always in front of me
2. Because He is at my right hand, I will not be moved
3. My body will rest without fear
4. You will not give me over to the grave
5. You will show me the way of life
6. In Your presence is fullness of joy
7. In Your right hand there is happiness forever

Exit Invitatory Bead: My heart is glad and my soul is full of joy.

Exit Cross: You alone, Lord, make me dwell in safety.

Scripture References:
Psalm 16   Psalm 4:8

You Have Made Me Glad

Cross: Whom have I in heaven but You. There is none I desire beside You.

Invitatory Bead: I will bless You, Lord, forever. I will trust You at all times.

Cruciform Beads: I will not be moved.

Week Beads:
1. You are my shield
2. My strength
3. My portion
4. Deliverer
5. My shelter
6. Strong tower
7. My very present help in time of need

Exit Invitatory Bead: You have delivered me from all fear. You have set my feet upon a rock.

Exit Cross: You have made me glad.

Scripture References:

Psalm 34	Psalm 40	Psalm 16:8
Psalm 18	Psalm 142:5	Psalm 46

Spiritual Warfare

Cross: Whoever calls upon the name of the Lord will be delivered and saved.

Invitatory Bead: When I cry unto You, then my enemies turn back: this I know; for You are for me.

Cruciform Beads: You will go before me, and You, oh God of Israel, will be my rear guard.

Week Beads:
1. Though I walk in the flesh, I do not war according to the flesh
2. The weapons of my warfare are not of the flesh
3. They are divinely powerful for the destruction of fortresses
4. I am destroying speculations
5. I am demolishing every lofty thing raised up against the knowledge of God
6. I take every thought captive to the obedience of Christ
7. I stand against the devil which causes him to run away from me

Exit Invitatory Bead: No weapon formed against me will prosper and every tongue that rises up against me in judgment will be condemned.

Exit Cross: I am from You, and have overcome my enemies because greater are You within me, than the one who is in the world.

Scripture References:

Joel 2:32	Psalm 56:9	Isaiah 52:2
2 Corinthians 10:3-5	Isaiah 54:7	1 John 4:4
James 4:7		

Prayer For Pastors

Cross: Lord, I ask You to fill my pastors with the knowledge of Your will, living a life worthy of You, pleasing You in every way, bearing fruit in every good work, growing in the knowledge of You, strengthened with all power according to Your glorious might, having great endurance and patience, and joyfully giving thanks to You.

Invitatory Bead: I respond to the urge, by You, Lord Jesus Christ, and by the love of Your Spirit, to join in my pastor's struggle by praying to You for them.

Cruciform Beads: Open the floodgates of heaven and pour out good things for my pastors until there is no more need.

Week Beads: I lift before You:
1. their ministry
2. their relationship with the Lord
3. their relationships with the congregation and the community
4. their leadership, guidance and direction
5. their protection, health and wholeness
6. their stewardship and priorities
7. their family

Exit Invitatory: I pray that my pastors would be wise in the way they act toward outsiders; making the most of every opportunity.

Exit Cross: I pray that in all respects my pastors prosper and be in good health, just as their souls prosper.

Scripture References:
Colossians 1:9-12   Romans 15:30   Malachi 3:10
Colossians 4:5-6   3 John 1:2

The Prayer of a Wife

Cross: The Lord God said, "It is not good that man should be alone; I will make him a helper comparable to him.

Invitatory Bead: I am a garden enclosed, a spring shut up, a fountain sealed for my husband alone. Many waters cannot quench my love for my husband, nor can the floods drown it.

Cruciform Beads: In the hidden person of my heart I adorn myself with the incorruptible beauty of a gentle and quiet spirit, which is very precious in Your sight, O God.

Week Beads:
1. My husband's heart safely trusts me
2. I will do him good and not evil all the days of my life
3. Strength and honor are my clothes
4. I rejoice when I look at the future
5. I open my mouth with wisdom and on my tongue is the law of kindness
6. The bread of idleness (gossip, discontent and self-pity) I refuse to eat
7. My children rise up and call me blessed, my husband praises me, also

Exit Invitatory Bead: I will be satisfied with good by the fruit of my mouth and the recompense of my hands will be rendered to me.

Exit Cross: My desire shall be for my husband and I submit to him as unto the Lord.

Scripture References:

Genesis 2:18	Song of Solomon 4:12	Song of Solomon 8:7
1 Peter 3:3-4	Proverbs 31:11-28	Proverbs 12:14
Ephesians 5:22		

I Am

Cross: I am alive with Christ even though I was dead in transgressions.

Invitatory Bead: I am invited to approach the throne of our merciful God.

Cruciform Beads: I am a new creation

Week Beads:
1. I am God's child
2. I am free from condemnation
3. I am accepted because of Christ
4. I am healed by the wounds Jesus bore
5. I am a friend of Jesus Christ
6. I am able to do all things through Christ who gives me strength
7. I am the light of the world

Exit Invitatory Bead: I am forgiven of all my sins

Exit Cross: I am the righteousness of God in Jesus Christ

Scripture References:

Ephesians 2:5	Hebrews 4:16	2 Corinthians 5:17
John 1:12	Romans 8:1-2	Romans 5:9
1 Peter 2:21	John 15:15	Ephesians 4:13
Matthew 5:14	Ephesians 1:7	2 Corinthians 5:21

The Tree

Cross: The Lord's Prayer

Invitatory Bead: Psalm 23

Cruciform Beads: Lord, You are in control and You can be trusted.

Week Beads:
1. I am like a tree replanted in Eden
2. Putting down roots near the river
3. Never anxious even in the hottest of summers
4. Never dropping a leaf
5. Serene and calm in drought
6. Bearing fresh fruit every season
7. Everything I put my hands to will prosper

Exit Invitatory Bead: Psalm 23

Exit Cross: The Lord's Prayer

The Lord's Prayer: Our Father, Who art in heaven, hallowed be Thy name. Thy Kingdom come, Thy will be done on earth as it is in heaven. Give us this day our daily bread, and forgive us our sins as we forgive those who sin against us. Lead us not into temptation, but deliver us from evil; for Thine is the Kingdom and the power and the glory forever. Amen.

Psalm 23: The Lord is my Shepard, I shall not want. He makes me to lie down in green pastures. He leads me beside still waters. He restores my soul. He leads me in paths of righteousness for His name's sake. Even though I walk through the Valley of the Shadow of Death, I will fear no evil; for Thou art with me. Thy rod and thy staff they comfort me. You prepare a table before me in the presence of my enemies. My cup runs over. Surely goodness and mercy shall follow me all the days of my life and I will dwell in the house of the Lord forever.

Scripture References:
Jeremiah 17:7-8   Psalm 1:3   Matthew 6:10-13   Psalm 23

My Prayer

(This space is given for you to develop your own personal prayer.)

Cross:

Invitatory Bead:

Cruciform Beads:

Week Beads:
1.

2.

3.

4.

5.

6.

7.

Exit Invitatory Bead:

Exit Cross:

Scripture References:

My Prayer
(This space is given for you to develop your own personal prayer.)

Cross:

Invitatory Bead:

Cruciform Beads:

Week Beads:
1.

2.

3.

4.

5.

6.

7.

Exit Invitatory Bead:

Exit Cross:

Scripture References:

ABOUT THE EDITOR

Tami serves as a Literacy Specialist with Pioneer Bible Translators. Pioneer Bible Translators' vision is to see networks of churches using God's Word in their own language to transform lives and build His Kingdom here on earth. Tami's passion is to see mother-tongue speakers fully utilizing the translated materials available to them. Her mission is to enable the Bibleless to read God's Word in their heart language, understand it, and apply its transforming power to their lives. She works from her home office in Michigan, and also regularly travels to East Africa to facilitate vernacular language programs and conduct literacy training events.

Proceeds from this booklet are used to support Tami's work with Pioneer Bible Translators. For information on purchasing sets of Anglican Prayer Beads, contact Tami at tami.allen@pbti.org.

Made in United States
Troutdale, OR
07/28/2023

11635488R00033